D0854335

MARC TIME

The Best of Marc

HODDER AND STOUGHTON

To Anna

British Library Cataloguing in Publication Data

Marc
    Marc time.
    1. English wit and humour, Pictorial
    Rn: Mark Boxer   I. Title
    741.5'942   NC1479

ISBN 0-340-36288-X

Printed in Great Britain for Hodder and Stoughton Limited,
Mill Road, Dunton Green, Sevenoaks, Kent by Hazell,
Watson & Viney Ltd., Aylesbury.

Hodder and Stoughton Editorial Office: 47 Bedford Square,
London WC1B 3DP

The Guardian June 16th 1983

Introduction

The present collection of cartoons start with Mrs
Thatcher's campaign for re-election. Since then
the high points from a cartoonist's point of view
have been the engrossing lapse and subsequent
wrigglings of Mr Cecil Parkinson, the coming to
further manhood of Prince Andrew, and the
androgynous swoopings of Torvill and Dean
whose Olympic win was rewarded with a
congratulatory telegram from the
director-general of the Arts Council. Mark
Thatcher appears to have gone to Oman; Sarah
Tisdall was offered a job by the *Guardian*.
Football managers left their wives even quicker
than they were sacked; Rats of various kinds
dominated TVam. Tiny Rowland and Robert
Maxwell breakfasted together; Arthur Scargill
and Mr MacGregor didn't.

    All this is daily fodder for the cartoonist.
Though the stories linger on, most of the cartoons
last little longer than a day. Indeed when I
worked for the *Times* some were dropped during
the night. This usually meant that the cartoon in
question was a success and had hit a certain
nerve. No such indicator now exists. The
selection is therefore a personal one of cartoons I
would like to see preserved rather than
rediscovered lining cupboards.

    My thanks are due to the editor of the
Guardian and his colleague, Mike McNay, for
their encouragement; to Smirnoff and their
advertising agency, Young & Rubicam and to
Sarah Smith there, who have proved the most
open-minded and sympathetic of patrons; and to
my editor at Hodder & Stoughton, Ion Trewin,
for this confidence. Finally to my collaborator,
George Melly for his many ideas and for
enlivening an inevitably solitary occupation.

M.B.

'Do you remember the first time you wrapped yourself in a newspaper announcing the recession was bottoming out?'

'If you sleep with me, I promise not to get you a job in TVam'

General election announced
The Guardian May 17th 1983

The Guardian June 1st 1983

The Guardian June 3rd 1983

'Tell me, colonel, which Lady Di look-alike is your son?'

'Shall we stop here where it's "disgusting", or push on thirty miles where it's "poor"?'

'Mr Koestler is coming through. He wants *me* to have the chair in parapsychology'

The Guardian June 22nd 1983

'Richman, poorman, criminal,
terrorist . . .'

'He hasn't got any job prospects, Daddy, but he's been libelled by Private Eye'

The Guardian July 13th 1983

'If you can't get to sleep, imagine you're
a line judge . . .'

The Guardian July 21st 1983

'Will you get out of bed; I want you to be one of the 8 per cent who propose on their knees'

The Guardian July 27th 1983

'All right. If you behave for the rest of the journey, mummy promises not to go topless when we get there'

'For heaven's sake, Ken, let them finish painting the lounge before revealing you are joining the dole fraud squad'

The Guardian August 10th 1983

The Guardian September 1st 1983

'The rehearsal was terrible, darling; but it'll be marvellous for the memoirs'

The Guardian September 27th 1983

'Are you signing on in London or the country?'

The Guardian September 30th 1983

The Guardian October 3rd 1983

'I've got this great way of sticking to my diet – I *insist* on seeing the kitchen before I order'

'Don't say two timing, sweetie; think of it as time sharing'

The Guardian November 4th 1983

'Swab . . . forceps . . ., Dr Jonathan
Miller's pop-up book . . .'

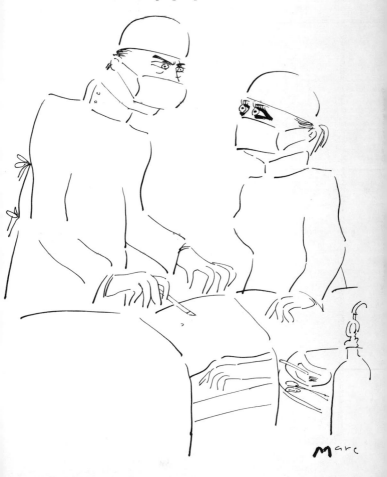

'I was going to divorce Guy, but if this bill goes through I might just settle for a reconciliation'

Revised divorce bill favouring men
proposed by Lord Hailsham and others

The Guardian November 8th 1983

'Trevor seems rather backward, doctor.
He can't switch on his own video nasty'

The Guardian December 3rd 1983

'There's one consolation – no office party . . .'

The Guardian December 8th 1983

Another MP discloses an affair

The Guardian December 14th 1983

'Instead of a black pudding, Mother, we'd love a copy of the Radio Times . . .'

Dispute stops southern edition of *Radio Times*
The Guardian December 23rd 1983

'We can't go on meeting like this; my husband has been made redundant . . .'

'I think I ought to tell you, sweetie,
we've got a little front page story
on the way'

Photographs of Sara Keay's baby published
The Guardian January 12th 1984

The Guardian January 13th 1984

'Yes, we're getting an annulment; Charles went to see Monsignor in a wheelchair'

Catholic church refuses wedding to crippled man
The Guardian January 25th 1984

'. . . £75 a week; and my friend and I guarantee no sexual harassment'

'Can you send round a little man at once? The cistern's leaking like a cabinet minister'

The Guardian February 8th 1984

'Apparently he tried to smile at number two camera'

The Guardian February 10th 1984

Chesterfield by-election
The Guardian February 24th 1984

'We didn't mind when we heard Sharon was going out with a weight lifter; but then we found out it was a woman . . .'

The Guardian February 29th 1984

'I'm sorry, we can't call it both Torvill *and* Dean'

The Guardian March 6th 1984

'That lot went for tits and bums in the
Daily Star, and that lot went for Derek
Jameson's libel case'

'Have you tried the Barbican?'

'The family feels, doctor, it's now alright to switch off grandfather's support machine'

The Lawson budget

The Guardian March 15th 1984

'Unfortunately our diva is unable to sing tonight due to a sore throat smoking our sponsor's product'

The Guardian March 27th 1984

The Guardian March 28th 1984

'When we're shareholders should we encourage Sophie to talk to her girlfriend in New York for hours?

The Guardian March 29th 1984

'Do you think it would be more fun if we ran a newspaper?'

The Guardian May 1st 1984

'He belongs to so many gay clubs, dear,
he must be a policeman'

MP arrested in gay club
The Guardian May 15th 1984

The Guardian May 16th 1984

The Guardian June 5th 1984

'At first we felt homesick; but then
Homer got mugged'

The Guardian June 13th 1984

The miners' strike continues
The Guardian June 20th 1984